VANCE BIBLIOGRAPHIES   Pub. Admin. Series: Bibliography #P 1635
                         ISSN: 0193-970X
                         ISBN: 0-89028-305-2

WAGE DETERMINATION AND COMPARABLE WORTH FOR LIBRARIANS:

A CHECKLIST OF MATERIALS

by

Lorna Peterson
Iowa State University Library
Ames, Iowa

Comparable worth is the theory that the marketplace discriminates against women by establishing lower rates of compensation for occupations dominated by females. This institutionalized sexism results in lower pay of females than is received by males in occupations which require comparable levels of education, skills, difficulty and safety.

Librarians are no strangers to the concept of comparable worth and its implementation. Long aware of the inequities in the marketplace, librarians have scrutinized the economic issues effecting them. Librarians have been instrumental in the enforcement activity and litigation concerning the Equal Pay Act and other legislation regarding pay equity in the attempt to achieve comparable worth in the marketplace.

The following bibliography is a selective checklist of materials on wage determination and comparable worth for librarians. Items cover the period 1970 - June 1984. For excellent annotated bibliographies on this topic see The Role of Women in Librarianship 1876-1979: The entry, advancement, and struggle for equalization in one profession and its companion volume, On Account of Sex: An annotated bibliography on the status of women in librarianship 1977-1981.

I. PAY EQUITY, COMPARABLE WORTH AND AFFIRMATIVE ACTION: A BRIEF LIST

"AIM Profiles the Information Management Professional." Information Manager. Spring 1980, pp. 32-33.

"ALA Favors Pay Equity Bills, Rejects OPM Monitoring." American Libraries. June 1984, p. 361.

"ARL Issues Salary Survey." Wilson Library Bulletin. February 1981, pp. 407-408.

American Federation State, County and Municipal Employees. Pay Equity: A union issue for the 1980's. Washington, D.C.

American Library Association. Office for Library Personnel Resources. Pay Equity: Comparable worth action guide. Chicago: American Library Association, 1981.

American Library Association. Social Responsibilities Round Table Task Force on the Status of Women. Women in a Woman's Profession: Strategies. Preconference on the status of Women in Librarianship. Chicago: American Library Association, 1984.

"An Analytical Approach to Salary Evaluation for Educational Personnel." International Journal of Education Sciences. October 1969, pp. 161-172.

"Another Equal Pay Complaint Filed by Canadian Libraries." Library Journal. July 1981, p. 1372.

Ballard, Robert, et al. Equal Pay for Equal Work: Women in special libraries. New York: Special Libraries Association. Special Committee on the Pilot Education Project, 1981.

Bearman, D. "1982 Survey of the Archival Profession." American Archivist. Spring 1983, pp. 233-41.

Berzins, B. "Australian Society of Archivists Survey of Salaries and Conditions of Employment." Archives and Manuscripts: Journal of the Australian Society of Archivists. May 1982, pp. 53-63.

Bidlack, R. E. "Some Economic and Demographic Realities Facing Library Education." Public Library Quarterly. Spring 1983, pp. 5-15.

Bird, Caroline. Born Female: The high cost of keeping women down. New York: McKay, 1968.

Bird, Caroline. *Everything a Woman Needs to Know to Get Paid What She's Worth.* New York: McKay, 1973.

Byerly, Greg. "The Faculty Status of Academic Librarians in Ohio." *College and Research Libraries.* September 1980, pp. 422-429.

"Canada Sex Bias Complaint Dismissed on a Technicality." *Library Journal.* February 1, 1982, p. 214.

"Canadian Federal Librarians Win Bias Back Pay." *Library Journal.* March 15, 1981, p. 601.

"Canadians Win Equal Pay for Work of Equal Value." *American Libraries.* April 1981, pp. 175-176.

Chen, Donna H.C. with assistance of Anne Boaxton. "Wage Determination for Librarians: Current status and future needs." Unpublished paper presented at Academic Library Association of Ohio meeting, October 1984.

Cleaver, Elaine. "Comparable Worth for Librarians." In *Manual on Pay Equity.* Washington, D.C.: Conference Publications, 1981, pp. 171-172.

Comparable Pay Study of the City and County of San Francisco, A Joint Project of the Women Library Workers and the Commission on the Status of Women. February 1978. Women Library Workers, P. O. Box 9052, Berkeley, California 94709.

Comparable Worth: A symposium on the issues and alternatives, proceedings of November 21, 1980. Washington, D.C.: Equal Employment Advisory Council, 1981.

The Comparable Worth Issue. Washington, D.C.: BNA Books, 1981.

"'Comparable Worth' Ruling: Compliance advised by report." *Library Journal.* March 1, 1984, p. 412.

"Comparable Worth Study Upgrades Oregon Librarians." *Library Journal.* April 15, 1984, p. 751.

Cook, Alice Hanson. *Comparable Worth, the Problem and States' Approaches to Wage Equity.* Honolulu, Hawaii: Industrial Relations Center, University of Hawaii at Manoa, 1983.

Cook, E. H. *Comparable Worth.* Monticello, Illinois: Vance Bibliographies, 1983. (Public Administration Series: Bibliographies #P 1321).

Cornell University. Libraries Committee on the Economic Status of Librarians. "8th Report to the Academic Assembly 1978/79 - 1979/80." Cornell University Library Bulletin. September 1979, pp. 16-26.

"Decade's $$ Problems Grip ARL Libraries." Library Journal. February 15, 1981, pp. 413-414.

Defichy, W. "Affirmative Action: Equal opportunity for women in library management." College and Research Libraries. May 1973, pp. 195-201.

Deutrich, M. E. and B. DeWhitt. "Survey of the Archival Profession - 1979." American Archivist. Fall 1980, pp. 527-535.

Drake, S. "Kuinka Kirjastonhoitajan ammatista tuli naisvaltainen ja alipalkattu (How Librarianship Became Woman's Work, and Underpaid)." Kirjastolehti. 1980, pp. 372-374.

Dworaczek, Marian. Equal Pay for Comparable Work: A bibliography. Monticello, Illinois: Vance Bibliographies, 1984. (Public Administration Series: Bibliography #P 1476).

"Equal Employment Opportunity: Affirmative action plans for libraries." American Libraries. October 1971, pp. 977-983.

Estes, M. E. "Southern California Association of Law Libraries 1979 Salary Survey: Another regional reflection of a national pattern?" Law Library Journal. Summer 1979, pp. 526-533.

"Factor Effecting Variations in Faculty Salaries and Compensation in Institutions of Higher Education." Journal of Higher Education. February 1973, pp. 124-136.

"Fairfax County Librarians File Pay Equity Complaint." American Libraries. June 1983, p. 334.

Farley, Jennie. Affirmative Action and the Woman Worker: Guidelines for personnel management. New York: Amacom, 1979.

"Financial Concessions at Detroit Public." Wilson Library Bulletin. September 1982, p. 15.

Fischer, R. G. "Pay Equity and the San Jose Strike: An interview with Patt Curia." Library Journal. November 1, 1981, pp. 2079-2085.

Gafarova, Z. "Khochetsia rabotat' luchshe (Better work is expected)." Bibliotekar'. 1977, p. 3.

Galloway, Sue. "Discrimination and Affirmative Action: Concerns for women librarians and library workers." In Librarians Affirmative Action Handbook. Metuchen, New Jersey: Scarecrow Press, 1983, pp. 154-176.

Galloway, Sue and Alyce Archuletai. "Sex and Salary: Equal pay for Comparable Work." American Libraries, May 1978, pp. 281-285.

Garcia, L. C. "Legal Services Law Librarianship--An investigation of salary and benefits in a pioneer field." Law Library Journal. Summer 1980, pp. 731-733.

Gassaway, Laura N. "Comparable Worth: A post-Gunther overview." The Georgetown Law Journal. June 1981, pp. 1123-1169.

Gellatly, P. "Are Serialists Underpaid?" Serials Librarian. Winter 1978, pp. 115-117.

Gill, P. "Responsibility the Key to Radical New Salary Approach." Library Association Record. May 1982, p. 187.

Gold, Michael Evan. A Dialogue on Comparable Worth. Ithaca, New York: ILR Press: New York State School of Industrial and Labor Relations, Cornell University, 1983.

Grune, Joy Ann, ed. Manual on Pay Equity: Raising wages for women's work. Washington, D.C.: Conference Publications, 1981.

Heim, Kathleen. "The Demographic and Economic Status of Librarians in the 1970's with Special References to Women." In Advances in Librarianship. V.12. New York: Academic Press, 1982.

Heim, Kathleen M. and Leigh S. Estabrook. Career Profiles and Sex Discrimination in the Library Profession. Chicago: American Library Association, 1983.

Heim, Kathleen M. and K. Phenix. "Comparison of Children and Adult Services Librarians' Salaries in LACONI." Illinois Libraries. December 1982, pp. 1160-1168.

Heim, Kathleen M. and Katherine Phenix. On Account of Sex: An Annotated Bibliography on the Status of Women in Librarianship, 1977-1981. Chicago: American Library Association, 1984.

Heim, Kathleen and Carolyn Kacena. "Sex, Salaries and Library Support." Library Journal. January 1, 1980, pp. 17-22.

Heim, Kathleen M. "Toward a Workforce Analysis of the School Library Media of the School Library Media Professional." School Media Quarterly. Summer 1981, pp. 235-249.

Henderson, Richard I. and Kitty Lewis Clarke. Job Pay for Job Worth: Designing and managing an equitable job classification and pay system. Atlanta, Georgia: Business Pub. Division, College of Business Administration, Georgia State University, 1981.

Hendrickson, Robert M. and Barbara A. Lee. "Academic Employment and Retrenchment: Judicial review and administrative action." ERIC Document ED 240 972. 1983.

Holman, Norman. "Comparable Worth and Library Employment." Drexel Library Quarterly. Summer 1981, pp. 27-34.

"Increased Productivity Ups Salaries for SDPL (San Diego Public Library) Staff." Library Journal. July 1982, p. 1278.

Jongeward, Dorothy and Dru Scott. Affirmative Action for Women: A practical guide for women and management. Reading, Massachusetts: Addison-Wesley, 1975.

Josephine, Helen B. "Women's Wages: Materials on pay equity." Collection Building. November 14, 1983, pp. 68-72.

Josephine, Helen B. "All Things Being Equal: Pay equity for library workers." Wilson Library Bulletin. December 1982, pp. 300-303.

Josephine, Helen B. "Up Your Wages (pay parity)." Women Library Workers Journal. July 1982, pp. 4-5.

Klement, Susan. "Feminism and Professionalism in Librarianship: An interview with Sherrill Cheda." Canadian Library Journal. December 1974, pp. 520-528.

Klett, R. and K. Seawell. "Tar Heel Enclove: Public library salaries in North Carolina." North Carolina Libraries. Spring 1983, pp. 15-22.

Koch, James V. and John F. Chizman. The Economics of Affirmative Action. Lexington, Massachusetts: Lexington Books, 1976.

Kronus, C. L. and J. W. Grimm. "Women in Librarianship: The majority rules?" Protean. December 1971, pp. 4-9.

Learmont, C. L. and S. Van Houten. "Placements and Salaries 1980: Holding the line." Library Journal. October 1, 1981, pp. 1881-1887.

Learmont, C. L. and S. Van Houten. "Placements and Salaries 1981: Still Holding." Erratum Library Journal. January 1, 1982, p. 2.

Learmont, C. L. and S. Van Houten. "Placements and Salaries 1981: Still Holding." Library Journal. October 1, 1982, pp. 1821-1827.

Learmont, C. L. and S. Van Houten. "Placements and Salaries 1982: Slowing Down." Library Journal. September 15, 1982, pp. 1760-1766.

Levy, Claudia. "Comparable Worth May Be Rights Issue of 80's." Washington Post. October 13, 1980, Bus. Sec. p. 3.

"Librarians Cut Salaries 4% to Save Jobs and Services." American Libraries. July 1982, p. 445.

"Librarians Win $905,000 in Sex Discrimination Case at University of Minnesota." American Libraries. June 1983, p. 337.

"Library Lawsuit Centers on Minimum Qualification." American Libraries. July/August 1981, p. 339.

Livernash, E. Robert, ed. Comparable Worth: Issues and alternatives. Washington, D.C.: Equal Employment Advisory Council, 1980.

Lloyd, K. R. "Working Woman: Leadership for the 80's." North Caroline(?) Libraries. Winter 1981, pp. 31-37.

"MLA Up Minimum Salary." Library Journal. October 1, 1980, p. 2024.

"Median Salary Reaches $23,500 Academic Library Survey Reports." American Libraries. March 1983, pp. 118-119.

"Minimum Starting Salary Recommendations for Public Libraries 1983." New Jersey Libraries. Fall 1983, pp. 36-37.

Mutari, E., et al. "Equal Pay for Work of Comparable Value." Special Libraries. April 1982, pp. 108-117.

Myers, M. "Recent Library Personnel Surveys." In Bowker Annual of Library Book Trade Information. New York: Bowker, 1982.

Nelson, M. G. "ALA Executive Board Approves Hewitt Study at Fall Meeting." Wilson Library Bulletin. December 1983, pp. 249-251.

Nelson, M. G. "I'm Okay, You're Okay, But Are We Okay?" (Study of job classifications and salaries at ALA Headquarters). Wilson Library Bulletin. December 1982, pp. 300-303.

Nelson, M. G. "Voting Ourselves a Raise." Wilson Library Bulletin. May 1981, p. 644.

Nelson, W. D. "Federal Wage Rates and the GPO." Wilson Library Bulletin. September 1983, p. 42.

"New Salary Increases Will Hurt Enoch Pratt." Library Journal. March 1, 1981, p. 503.

"1980 Median Salary $19,700 for SLA Members Up 9.4%." American Libraries. February 1981, p. 64.

"1982 Minimum Starting Salary Recommendations." New Jersey Libraries. Fall 1981, pp. 2-3.

"Ninth Library School Survey: Changes at helm, gains for women." Library Journal. October 1, 1982, pp. 1803-1804.

"North Dakota Legislature Up Salaries in Academe." Library Journal. March 1, 1981, p. 503.

Pearson, L. R. "Library Workers Lead Strikers in Comparable-pay Fight." American Libraries. July/August 1981, p. 397.

Pezzullo, Thomas R. and Barbara E. Brittingham, eds. Salary Equity: Detecting sex bias in salaries among college and university professors. Lexington, Massachusetts: Lexington Book, 1979.

Prostano, E. T. "Salaries of M.L.S. Graduates 1980." Connecticut Libraries. Fall 1981, p. 12.

"Public/School Library Parity Sought for N.C. Librarians." Library Journal. May 1, 1984, pp. 845-846.

Reid, M. T. "Professional Salaries in Louisiana Academic Libraries, 1980-1981." Louisiana Library Association Bulletin. Fall 1982, pp. 82-85.

Remick, Helen. Comparable Worth and Wage Discrimination: Technical Possibilities and Political Realities. Philadelphia: Temple University Press, 1984.

"Report on Studying the Feasibility of Adopting a Minimum Salary for Librarians." New Jersey Libraries. April 1980, pp. 15-18.

"Rhode Island Endorses Minimum Salary." Wilson Library Bulletin. April 1983, p. 633.

"Rhode Island Library Association Sets Minimum Salary for Librarians." Library Journal. May 1, 1983, p. 868.

Rowley, J. E. and M. Wallis. "Law Mobility Evident, But Our Experiment Needs Refining." Library Association Record. October 1981, p. 505.

Safran, Claire. "The Issue of the 80's: Equal pay for comparable work." Redbook. November 1981, pp. 78, 153.

"Salaries Up, But Variance Still High." College and Research Libraries News. May 1981, p. 142.

"Salary Gains Recorded for ARL Librarians." College and Research Libraries News. June 1980, p. 178.

"Salary Survey: A Vermont Department of Libraries survey conducted in late 1977." NELA Newsletter. June 1978, p. 3.

Schiller, A. R. "Women in Librarianship." In Advances in Librarianship. V. 4, M. J. Voight, ed. New York: Academic Press, 1974.

Schuman, Patricia Glass. "Women, Power and Libraries." Library Journal. January 1, 1984, pp. 42-47.

Schwartz, Carolyn. A Bibliography of Materials Collected for Comparable Wages for Comparable Worth Study. Chicago: American Library Association, n.d.

Selden, C., E. Mutari, M. Rubin and K. Sacks. Equal Pay for Work of Comparable Worth: An annotated bibliography. Chicago: American Library Association, 1982.

Serov, V. V. "Novaia Zabota partii" (Party's new concern). Bibliotekar'. 1977, pp. 27-28.

"Sex and Salary Survey: Selected statistics of large public libraries in the United States and Canada." Library Journal. November 15, 1972, pp. 3682-3685.

"Sex Discrimination Complaint: Professional librarians at Temple University have filed a class action complaint." Herald Library Science. October 1977, p. 448.

Sharma, Prabha. "A Survey of Academic Librarians and Their Opinions Related to Nine-month Contracts and Academic States Configurations in Alabama, Georgia, and Mississippi." College and Research Libraries. November 1981, pp. 561-570.

Shediac, M. "Private Law Libraries, Special Interest Section, 1980 Salary Survey." Law Library Journal. Spring 1981, pp. 444-457.

"Should ALA Establish a Lowest-recommended Salary for Professional Librarians? A report on discussions to date." American Libraries. May 1980, pp. 291-292.

Simpson, William A. and William E. Sperber. "The Effects of Academic Market Value on the Outliers of a Multi-variant Regression Analysis of Faculty Salaries." ERIC Document ED 240 899. 1983.

"SLA 1983 Salary Survey Update." Special Libraries. October 1983, pp. 390-391.

"SLA Salaries Climb to $24,340 Average in 1982." American Libraries. June 1983, p. 338.

Smart, Anne. "Women--the 4/5 minority." Canadian Library Journal. February 1975, pp. 14-17.

Sonnemann, S. S. and J. L'Esperance. "Case of Discrimination." Canadian Library Journal. February 1983, pp. 9-12.

Special Libraries Association. "SLA 1982 Salary Survey; Draft report." Special Libraries. October 1982, pp. 314-315.

"Stone Battles Latest Threat to Librarian Status, Pay Equity." American Libraries. November 1982, pp. 613-614.

Stromberg, Ann H. and Shirley Harkness, eds. Women Working: Theories and facts in perspective. Palo Alto, California: Mayfield Pub. Co., 1978.

"Teaching and Publishing as Determinants of Academic Salaries." Journal of Economic Education. Spring 1973, pp. 90-99.

Thomas, D. A. "1980 Statistical Survey of Law School Libraries and Librarians." Law Library Journal. Spring 1981, pp. 359-443.

Thomas, D. A. "1979 Statistical Survey of Law School Libraries and Librarians." Law Library Journal. Spring 1980, pp. 451-497.

Treiman, Donald J. and Heidi I. Hartmann, eds. Women, Work and Wages: Equal pay for jobs of equal value. Washington, D.C.: National Research Council. Committee on Occupational Classification and Analysis. Assembly of Behavioral and Social Sciences, 1981.

"U. of Minnesota Pays $19,647 to Beginning Librarians." American Libraries. March 1982, p. 162.

United States. Bureau of Labor Statistics. Women at Work: A chartbook. Bulletin 2168. ERIC Document ED 237726, April 1983.

United States. Congress. House. Committee on Education and Labor. Special Subcommittee on Education. Discrimination Against Women: Congressional hearings on equal rights in education and employment. Catherine R. Stimpon, ed. New York: Bowker, 1973.

United States. Department of Labor. Laws on Sex Discrimination in Employment. Washington, D.C.: Department of Labor, 1970.

United States. Women's Bureau. Laws and Sex Discrimination in Employment: Federal Civil Rights Act, Title VII, State Fair Employment Practices, Laws, Executive Order. Washington, D.C.: Women's Bureau, 1973.

University of California, Berkeley. Library Affirmative Action for Women Committee. A Report on the Status of Women Employed in the Library of the University of California, Berkeley with the Recommendation for Affirmative Action. Berkeley: University of California, Berkeley, 1971. (ERIC Document ED 066 163).

University of Minnesota Librarians Win Sex Bias Case." Library Journal. June 1, 1983, pp. 1072-1074.

Wahba, Susanne Patterson. "Women in Libraries: Part I - Job satisfaction of librarians, a comparison between men and women. Part II - Women in libraries: A longitudinal study of career pay of men and women librarians." Law Library Journal. May 1976, pp. 228-231.

Weatherford, John. "Collective Bargaining and the Academic Librarian." Library Journal. February 15, 1980, pp. 481-482.

Weibel, Kathleen and Kathleen M. Heim. The Role of Women in Librarianship 1876-1976: The entry, advancement, and struggle for equalization in one profession. Phoenix: Oryx Press, 1979.

Wells, M. B. "Requirements and Benefits for Academic Librarians: 1959-1979." College and Research Libraries. November 1982, pp. 450-458.

Westerman, Mel. "Salary Comparisons Between Academic Librarians and Instructional Faculty." College and Research Libraries. July 1982, pp. 346-351.

Whitebook, Marcy and Willa Pettygrove. "Salary Surveys: How? Why? Who? When? Where? How to conduct one in your community." ERIC Document ED 238 571, 1983.

Williamson, J. "Pay Equity for Librarians." New York Library Association Bulletin. May 1981, p. 10.

Women's Work has Just Begun: Legal problems of employing women in universities. Ann Arbor, Michigan: Institute of Continuing Legal Education, 1972.

II. SALARY SURVEYS: Only examples of various types of surveys are included. Titles in Sections I and II are mainly limited to surveys published since 1980.

A. National and Regional Surveys

Allen County Public Library. Statistics of Public Libraries in the United States and Canada Serving 100,000 Population or More. Fort Wayne: Indiana, 1958-, biennial.

American Library Association. Association of Specialized and Cooperative Library Agencies. Salary Data - State Library Agencies. Chicago: ALA, annual.

Association of Research Libraries. ARL Annual Salary Survey. Washington, D.C.: ARL, 1977/78-.

Educational Research Service, Inc. National Survey of Salaries and Wages in Public Schools. Arlington, Virginia: ERS, 1974/75-, annual.

Heim, K. M. and Carolyn Kacena. "Sex, Salaries and Library Support." Rev. version. Bowker Annual of Library and Book Trade Information. 25th ed. New York: Bowker, 1981, pp. 334-44.

Kim, Ung Chon. A Statistical Study of Factors Affecting Salaries of Academic Librarians at Medium-sized State-supported Universities in Five Midwestern States. Doc. Diss. Bloomington, Indiana: Indiana University, 1980.

Learmont, Carol L. "Placements and Salaries 1979: Wider horizon." Library Journal. November 1, 1981, pp. 2271-7. An annual survey, with different co-authors, appears in fall or winter issues of Library Journal.

Library Compensation Review. Tucson, Arizona: University of Arizona, Graduate Library School, Winter 1982-, quarterly.

Lynch, Mary Jo, Margaret Myers and Jeniece Guy. ALA Survey of Librarian Salaries. Chicago: ALA, 1982.

Special Library Association. SLA Triennial Salary Survey. New York, 1983.

"SLA 1981 Salary Survey Update." Special Libraries. October 1981, pp. 399-400.

Sandstedt, Carl R. Salary Survey: West-north-central states. St. Peters, Missouri: St. Charles City-County Library, annual.

Pub. Admin. Series: Bibliography #P 1635

II. B. STATEWIDE SURVEYS

Gill, Karlyle, B.K.L. Genova and Elliot Cole. A Study of Salary Determinants within the SUNY Librarians' Association between 1973 and 1974. Arlington, Virginia: ERIC, 1977. ED 134 189.

Michigan Library Association. Salary and Fringe Benefit Survey, 1982. Lansing, 1982.

Reid, M. T. "1978/79 Professional Salaries in Louisiana Academic Libraries." Louisiana Library Association Bulletin, Spring 1980, pp. 107+.

"Salary Survey: A Vermont Department of Libraries survey conducted in late 1977." NELA Newsletter, June 1978, p. 3.

"Study of Academic Library Salaries in California." College and Research Libraries News, November 1978, p. 303.

Wisconsin Association of Public Librarians. Salary and Fringe Benefit Survey. 1983.

Young, Arthur. A Study to Establish an Evaluation System for State of Iowa Merit Employment Systems Classification on the Basis of Comparable Worth. Statistical supplement. Final report. Des Moines, Iowa: Legislative Service Bureau, 1984.

C. INTERNATIONAL SURVEYS: A BRIEF LIST - The intention of this list is to show that comparable worth for librarians is an international concern. It is not a comprehensive list.

"Deltidsbibliotekarernes løn-og ansaettelsesvilkar (Part-time librarians' salary and contract demand)." Bogens Verden. 1978, pp. 20-22.

Gutzmann, H. "Diplom-Bibliothekar an offentilichen Bibliotheken; ein Beruf, der nicht mehr in das vorgegebene Tarifschema der Berufe des offentlichen Dienstes passt (certified librarians at public libraries; a profession that does not fit into the salary schedule for public service employees)." Buch und Bibliothek: Fachzeitschrift des Vereins der Bibliothekare an Offentlichen Buchereien. April 1979, pp. 348+.

Hazell, J. "Staff and Salaries in Australian University Libraries in 1981." Australian Academic and Research Libraries. June 1981, pp. 103-121.

Marti, R. L'evolution des salaires dans les bibliotheques suisses entre 1947 et 1979 (Evolution of salaries in Swiss libraries between 1947 and 1979 (text in French and German). Vereiniguny Schweizerischer Bibliothekare) Schweizerische Vereinigung fur Dokumentation Nachrichten. June 1980, pp. 103-109.

Marti, R. "Les salaires dans les bibliotheques swisses en 1979; enquete realisee par l'organisation du personnel de l'ABS (Salaries in Swiss libraries in 1979; an inquiry of the personnel organization of the Association of Swiss librarians (text in French and German). Vereinigung Schweizerischer Bibliothekare/Schweizerische Vereingung fur Dokumentation Nachrichten. April 1980, pp. 55-67.

III. WAGE THEORY: A BRIEF LIST

Adams, J. Stacy. "Towards an Understanding of Inequity," Journal of Abnormal and Social Psychology. 1963, pp. 422-436.

The American Society for Personnel Administration and the American Compensation Association. Elements of Sound Base Pay Administration. Berea, Ohio, 1981.

Brown, Henry Phelps. The Inequality of Pay. Berkeley: University of California Press, 1977.

Cartter, Allan M. Theory of Wages and Employment. Homewood, Illinois: Irwin, 1959.

Lawler, Edward E. Pay and Organization Development. Reading, Massachusetts: Addison-Wesley, 1981.

Mahoney, Thomas A. Compensation and Reward Perspective. Homewood, Illinois: Irwin, 1979.

Mahoney, Thomas A. "Organizational Hierarchy and Position Worth." Academy of Management Journal. 1979, pp. 726-37.

Rescher, Nicholas. Distributive Justice. New York: Bobbs-Merrill, 1966.

Taylor, George W., ed. New Concepts in Wage Determination. New York: McGraw-Hill, 1957.

Thurow, Lester C. Generating Inequality. New York: Basic Books, 1975.

Wallace, Marc and Charles Fay. Compensation Theory and Practice. Boston: Kent, 1983.

IV. COMPENSATION AND BENEFITS: A BRIEF LIST

Association of Research Libraries. Fringe Benefits in ARL Libraries. Spec. Kit no. 50. Washington, D.C., 1979.

Pub. Admin. Series: Bibliography #P 1635

Berg, J. Gary. Managing Compensation: Developing and administering the total compensation program. New York: American Management Associations, Inc., 1976.

Crandall, N. Frederic. "Wage and Salary Administrative Practices and Decision Process." Journal of Management. Spring 1979, pp. 71-90.

Dunn, J. D. and F. Rachel. Wage and Salary Administration: Total compensation systems. New York: McGraw-Hill, 1970.

Greene, Robert J. "Thoughts on Compensation Management in the 80s and 90s." Personnel Management. May 1980, pp. 27-28.

Hamilton, Eugene K. "How to Set Up Flexible Benefits." Compensation Review, First Quarter, 1982, pp. 68-74.

Jones, William G. Salary Compensation Systems for Librarians: A study of ten members of the Association of Research Libraries. Occasional paper, no. 5. Washington, D.C.: Association of Research Libraries, 1981.

Lawson, J. W. and Ballard Smith. Management's Complete Guide to Employee Benefits. Chicago: Dartnell Corp., 1980.

Miller, John J. "Trends and Practices in Employee Benefits." Personnel Administrator. May 1980, pp. 48-51+.

Rosenbloom, Jerry S., and Victor G. Hallman. Employee Benefit Planning. Englewood Cliffs, New Jersey: Prentice-Hall, 1981.

U.S. Office of Personnel Management. Integrated Salary and Benefits Programs for State and Local Government. Washington, D.C.: U.S. Government Printing Office, 1979.

White, William L. and James W. Becker. "Increasing the Motivational Impact of Employee Benefits." Personnel. January-February 1980, pp. 32-37.

V. RELEVANT EXECUTIVE ORDERS AND LEGISLATION BY THE UNITED STATES. A BRIEF CHRONOLOGICAL LISTING

Equal Pay Act of 1963.

Title VII. Civil Rights Act of 1964.

Executive Order 11246. October 13, 1968.

Executive Order 11478. August 12, 1969.

Equal Employment Opportunities Act of 1972.

VANCE BIBLIOGRAPHIES	Pub. Admin. Series: Bibliography #P 1635
	ISSN: 0193-970X
	ISBN: 0-89028-305-2

WAGE DETERMINATION AND COMPARABLE WORTH FOR LIBRARIANS:

A CHECKLIST OF MATERIALS

Additional copies available from:

VANCE BIBLIOGRAPHIES
Post Office Box 229
Monticello, Illinois 61856

for $2.25.

DATE DUE

284211